WALKING WITH Beasts

Survival!

Adapted by Stephen Cole

A NEW BEGINNING

It's 65 million years ago and a single rock, called a meteor, is shooting through space at 240,000 kilometres per hour. The meteor is nearly ten kilometres wide – so big, it would take an adult about an hour and a half to walk across it – and it's heading straight for the Earth…

When the meteor hits, the impact is worse than dozens of nuclear bombs. The blast sets off volcanoes, filling the air with deadly gases. Around 400 million, million tonnes of rock and dust are thrown into the sky. The dust clouds block out the sun, and acid rain pours down on the **dinosaurs'** ruined world.

Amazingly, some animals survive. They will eventually evolve into **mammals** just as weird and wonderful – just as varied in size, shape and behaviour – as the dinosaurs that came before them. But if you were among them, watching them, or being hunted by them … you might call these mammals BEASTS.

Leave the modern world behind and imagine yourself transported back in time. Prepare to meet these prehistoric creatures – come walking with beasts...

FOREST OF FEAR

You've arrived.

Open your eyes and take your first look at the world as it was 49 million years ago. You're standing in a tropical forest at dawn. It's hot, wet, and you're surrounded by strange sounds – the screeches and wails of local wildlife. You shiver as you realize that you have no idea what could make noises like these.

Suddenly, without warning, something comes crashing through the foliage. It's called a **Propalaeotherium**. But all *you* want to know is … will it eat you?

Propalaeotherium takes a drink of water

Freaky … there's a kind of cat-sized horse with large, nervous eyes staring at me. It doesn't look dangerous, it's just nibbling grapes from the forest floor.

Millions of years from now, this animal will evolve into the horse we know today…

Searching for food in the forest

Suddenly, you freeze. You saw the Propalaeotherium approaching but, from the crashing noises, it's clear that something a lot bigger, heavier, and far more frightening is coming closer … the tiny horse looks up at you in alarm. Before it can move a single step, a terrifying, man-sized bird appears from nowhere! **Gastornis**, the terror bird – and a descendent of the meat-eating dinosaurs – is after both of you!

49 MILLION YEARS AGO

36 MILLION YEARS AGO

24 MILLION YEARS AGO

3.2 MILLION YEARS AGO

1 MILLION YEARS AGO

30,000 YEARS AGO

Gastornis is as tall as a grown man, and ripples with muscles and thick feathers. Propalaeotherium tries to run, but it's no use. The bird's massive beak snaps the tiny horse's spine like a pencil. While Gastornis is busy ripping hunks of flesh from the horse's still-twitching carcass, you run for your life...

After a while, you stop near a still, silent lake. You don't dare run too far – what if you bump into another monster? But it's a far less scary sight you see now, as little **Leptictidium**, a fidgety creature that looks like a cross between a shrew and a large cat, comes scampering through the forest. This animal feasts on insects, so you're safe – for the moment.

Leptictidium carefully kicks leaves out of its way and nudges twigs aside as it scurries forward. There's a reason for this fussiness – Leptictidium can only outrun predators if it has a clear escape route back to its burrow.

As you watch, you hear a sudden splash behind you...

Leptictidium at large!

SILENT KILLERS

You spin round and stagger back. Leptictidium shoots back into the safety of the forest as a huge, dark shape lunges up from the still waters of the lake. **Ambulocetus**, a creepy creature that looks like a cross between a whale and a crocodile, lurks by the water's edge, waiting for something careless enough to wander into its range … something like you!

You dive desperately to one side as Ambulocetus's massive jaws swing shut – missing your face by centimetres.

The creature comes so close you can smell its stale, sickly breath. You glimpse the cold bloodlust in its eyes, but manage to move out of its path, just in time.

Ambulocetus's snappy, croc-like jaws

It's no good screaming for mercy if Ambulocetus's teeth start tearing into my flesh – the creature's got no ears! It picks up the vibrations of any approaching animals by resting its jaws on the ground. Speaking of vibrations, what's that?

A tremor shakes the forest, and you stare wildly about, but all is still again. Just another mini-earthquake. But why is Ambulocetus sinking back into the muddy water? Your heart misses a beat as you realize the beast is dead. The tremor released *another* silent killer – a cloud of poisonous gas that was trapped deep under the lake's waters. Now that it's escaped, the gas will leak through the forest, suffocating everything in its path.

It's time to get out of here!

49 MILLION YEARS AGO

36 MILLION YEARS AGO

24 MILLION YEARS AGO

3.2 MILLION YEARS AGO

1 MILLION YEARS AGO

30,000 YEARS AGO

DEADLY CROSSING

49 MILLION YEARS AGO

36 MILLION YEARS AGO

24 MILLION YEARS AGO

3.2 MILLION YEARS AGO

1 MILLION YEARS AGO

30,000 YEARS AGO

In your rush to escape, you've leaped forward to 36 million years ago. The world is still busy changing – the continents are moving closer together but are still separated by huge seas.

A shriek from above catches your attention. You're looking into the wide, furry face of humanity's earliest ancestor, the monkey-like **Apidium**. A group of them swings from the trees above the swamp, searching for fruit to fill their bellies.

Without warning, a sleek, rocket-shaped fish emerges from the swamp water – it's a shark, hungry for flesh. One Apidium screams as the shark's needle-sharp teeth rip into its body. You turn and run into the undergrowth, unable to watch. While the others huddle in the high branches shaking with fear, the shark pulls its prize underwater. Slowly the monkey victim's cries fade into gurgles.

...nding food can be a risky activity

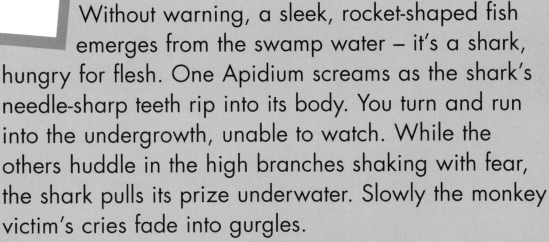

The swamp water stretches into the distance – there's no way I can safely reach any dry land. This mangrove swamp is eerily calm, but... is it my imagination, or is something shifting under the surface?

GENTLE BEASTS

You run until you reach a clearing in the swamp and see a herd of grazing **Brontotheres**. They look a little like rhinos, with a huge, heart-shaped slab of bone rising up from their squat, grey heads.

The Brontothere is the size of an elephant! There can't be many animals who would dare to pick a fight with this beast.

Despite their menacing looks, Brontotheres are peaceful plant-eaters. But as one of them shifts and stamps its massive foot, you notice it seems to be upset.

Then you spot the lifeless creature lying at the large beast's feet and you realize what's going on. The female Brontothere has just given birth to a dead calf, and the distraught mother emits a low wail of despair.

Brontothere mother with her dead calf at her feet

49 MILLION YEARS AGO

36 MILLION YEARS AGO

24 MILLION YEARS AGO

3.2 MILLION YEARS AGO

1 MILLION YEARS AGO

30,000 YEARS AGO

THE BODYSNATCHERS

A snarling **Andrewsarchus** approaches. Thick strings of drool hang from its mouth, forming pools around its paws. Now a second Andrewsarchus arrives and distracts the mother Brontothere, leaving its fellow **scavenger** free to grab at the baby's carcass. The hungry pair have found their next meal.

You edge away towards the prehistoric sea, drawn by the crashing of the waves against the nearby shore.

This beach is amazing – there are turtles everywhere! They've been laying eggs by the look of things. Oh, no! Here comes trouble again. A pack of Andrewsarchus has found the turtles – and me, too! I can't go back the way I came. They've cut me off, so there's only one way I can go to get away...

Andrewsarchus tucks in ...

49 MILLION YEARS AGO

36 MILLION YEARS AGO

24 MILLION YEARS AGO

3.2 MILLION YEARS AGO

1 MILLION YEARS AGO

30,000 YEARS AGO

HUNT AT SEA

As you splash through the water, you can't help remembering the shark – and how quickly it finished off the monkey-like Apidium back in the swamp. The water's cold, in spite of the heat of the day, but at last you reach a small island and crawl on to dry land, panting and choking after your swim.

49 MILLION YEARS AGO

36 MILLION YEARS AGO

24 MILLION YEARS AGO

3.2 MILLION YEARS AGO

1 MILLION YEARS AGO

30,000 YEARS AGO

A weird monster, looking a bit like a pig crossed with a hippopotamus, rises clumsily from the water and joins you on the sandbar, flicking its ears endearingly. It's an adult **Moeritherium**, a distant relative of the elephant. You can see how the upper lip that hangs down over its mouth will one day become a trunk, and how the sharp front teeth will eventually grow into tusks. But, right now, something's wrong. The Moeritherium seems frightened.

A moment later, you realize why. A **Basilosaurus**, the largest predator in the prehistoric seas, bursts into view. Its body is longer than a helicopter, its skull the size of a large sofa – and it intends to eat a whole Moeritherium for its dinner! Luckily, the big Basilosaurus can't swim in shallow water. While the Moeritherium breaks free, you dive back into the water – and swim for your life.

DEATHLY LAGOON

After a long, long swim, you reach the quiet, still waters of a lagoon. A splash ahead of you gives you a start – but there's no need for alarm this time. Dipping under water and holding your breath, you see hordes of baby dolphin-like creatures playing all around you. These wide-eyed wonders are called **Dorudon**. The mothers watch serenely as their young calves splash about.

Uh-oh! Something's stirred up the Dorudon... They're darting about as their mothers call and screech. The adults are frantically trying to steer their young to safety... Oh ... now I see why!

The massive, dark shape of the Basilosaurus looms up in the lagoon like a nuclear sub and moves just as quickly. The Dorudon scatter as the gigantic whale's 60-tonne bulk tears through the water. A group of calves panic and swim straight into its path. The Basilosaurus's jaws, 12 times as long as a crocodile's, swing shut on the soft flesh of the Dorudon young.

Shrill shrieks echo all around you and, suddenly, the clear, blue waters are turning red. Disgusted, you realize you can't hold your breath any longer. As you start to drift away from this period of time into a new age, the ghostly shadow of Basilosaurus returns to the open sea with its kill.

A baby Dorudon is just a snack to the giant Basilosaurus

49 MILLION YEARS AGO

36 MILLION YEARS AGO

24 MILLION YEARS AGO

3.2 MILLION YEARS AGO

1 MILLION YEARS AGO

30,000 YEARS AGO

BABY GIANT

When you return, it is ten million years later, and you find yourself in a quiet glade. The thick forests have opened up by 24 million years ago and, for the first time on your prehistoric journey, you see grass.

Ahead of you, on the dusty plain, you see a family of giants. An **Indricothere** calf towers above you. Unfortunately, someone else has spotted it, too. A menacing monster steals into view. Sleek and silent like a giant wolf, this is the scavenging **Hyaenodon**. The Indricothere mother bellows at the beast to keep back, but Hyaenodon stays put, hungrily watching and waiting for the mother to lower its guard.

With creatures like this around, how long can the defenceless calf survive?

You know there's nothing you can do, so you walk away into the woodlands.

The Hyaenodons plan their attack

49 MILLION YEARS AGO

36 MILLION YEARS AGO

24 MILLION YEARS AGO

3.2 MILLION YEARS AGO

1 MILLION YEARS AGO

30,000 YEARS AGO

Wow ... the newborn Indricothere calf's already the size of an armchair. It could easily squash me with one of those massive feet!

NEAR THE KNUCKLES

You come to a halt at the sound of a strange dragging, rustling noise coming from the trees. It's getting closer. Swallowing hard, you find somewhere to hide. The animal approaching is a **Chalicothere**, and the dragging noise is the sound of its knuckles scraping the ground as it shuffles along. As you watch from safety, you realize that the lumbering beast is far more interested in finding leaves to eat than in coming after you.

Chalicothere keeps a look-out for predators

Seconds later, you're glad of your hidey-hole. Another Hyaenodon darts from the bushes, throwing itself at the Chalicothere.

The air is thick with growls and roars, and splashes of blood fly around. More Hyaenodons turn up. Shocked, you turn to run. The only thing you can do in this savage world is try to keep alive ... and that means getting out of the way of this fight – and the next horrific monster that's approaching...

At first sight, I thought the Chalicothere looked quite cuddly – until the sunlight glinted on its sharp claws. But the Hyaenodons are the really vicious beasts.

49 MILLION YEARS AGO

36 MILLION YEARS

24 MILLION YEARS AGO

3.2 MILLION YEARS AGO

1 MILLION YEARS AGO

30,000 YEARS AGO

STAND-OFF

Meet **Entelodont**. A snarling monstrosity with a face like a pig and the bulk of a tank, it's not to be tangled with. The smell of fresh blood has brought it stampeding here, but the Hyaenodons don't look happy. You know there's going to be a fight over the poor Chalicothere's body. Sure enough, the Entelodont dashes over and starts ripping a leg from the bloodied carcass while a Hyaenodon snaps and howls at him to stop.

I can't bear this endless violence... I'm going to leap forward 21 million years, to the time of our earliest human ancestors. Surely, things will be a little calmer there. But first, there's just one more thing I want to see...

You return to the world five years later. You are on a dusty plain ringed by tall trees. It's sunset, and the sky is a deep, rich red. There's just one thing on your mind ... whatever happened to the baby Indricothere you saw?

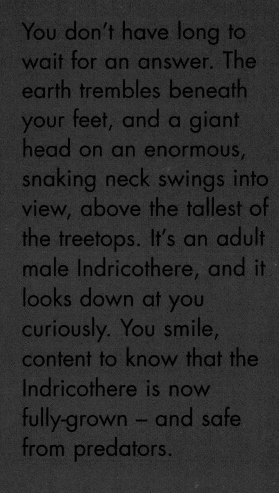

You don't have long to wait for an answer. The earth trembles beneath your feet, and a giant head on an enormous, snaking neck swings into view, above the tallest of the treetops. It's an adult male Indricothere, and it looks down at you curiously. You smile, content to know that the Indricothere is now fully-grown – and safe from predators.

Indricothere finds peace at last!

49 MILLION YEARS AGO

36 MILLION YEARS AGO

24 MILLION YEARS AGO

3.2 MILLION YEARS AGO

1 MILLION YEARS AGO

30,000 YEARS AGO

MᴇET THE ꜰAMILY

You open your eyes and find yourself in what will become Ethiopia, around three million years ago. You walk off into the forest to shelter from the blazing sun.

You came in search of humans but instead, you've found apes. **Australopithecus** are apes that walk on two legs. They live in groups, not because they want to be sociable – but simply to survive.

They're filthy animals, but if I were to trace back my family tree 150,000 generations, I'd probably end up here. The group leader is a huge, hairy creature with white tufts on his chin. I've nicknamed him Greybeard. I must seem a very strange kind of ape to him!

Before they can decide if you're friend or foe, another new arrival greets the troop – with a terrifying roar and a baring of teeth. Cries of fear and alarm go up from the panicking Australopithecus, as **Dinofelis**, a huge killer cat, races towards them…

49 MILLION YEARS AGO

36 MILLION YEARS AGO

24 MILLION YEARS AGO

3.2 MILLION YEARS AGO

1 MILLION YEARS AGO

30,000 YEARS AGO

DEATH CHARGE

A female Australopithecus falls down under the weight of the big cat, shrieking in terror. Her screams die away as Dinofelis's paws crush down on her windpipe and snap through her neck. The fierce feline leaves the clearing with the female's body between its teeth.

Greybeard throws a stone at the cat. It looks round briefly, eyes flashing with anger, then carries on. Greybeard and the others set off, following the big cat's tracks. They want to follow Dinofelis – and take revenge.

I keep my distance. Suddenly, I hear a murderous sound – the awesome bellow of **Deinotherium**, a giant elephant with curved tusks. It's been disturbed by the group and is preparing to charge...

Greybeard leads the fleeing troop to a huge, gnarled tree, which they swiftly scale. The ground shakes as Deinotherium rumbles closer. You try to climb up after the apes, but you can't get a good grip – and five tonnes of charging beast is almost upon you...

Deinotheruim charges
at the tree

49 MILLION YEARS AGO

36 MILLION YEARS AGO

24 MILLION YEARS AGO

3·2 MILLION YEARS AGO

1 MILLION YEARS AGO

30,000 YEARS AGO

THE STONING

Deinotherium rams the tree with its huge, grey head. There's a splintering crack as you're thrown clear, and you wonder if you've broken any bones.

Australopithecus fall around you, shaken from the tree like human coconuts. Together, you race for the cover of the trees. But the bellowing monster has made its point. It doesn't follow.

Greybeard picks up the trail again. He finds Dinofelis in its lair – a cool, dark cave. Greybeard hushes the others as you draw nearer. The Australopithecus stick together now. They gather bones from around the entrance to the cave – weapons for their revenge attack!

When Dinofelis emerges from the cave, the members of the troop start to scream, shout and to beat the killer cat with the bones. Dinofelis hisses in pain and anger, but there is no escape.

I turn away, sick at the savagery. Once again, it's time to leave...

49 MILLION YEARS AGO

36 MILLION YEARS AGO

24 MILLION YEARS

3.2 MILLION YEARS AGO

1 MILLION YEARS AGO

30,000 YEARS AGO

SA E-TOO

You're one million years from home, in what will one day be Paraguay in South America. Right now, it's just another grassy plain in a planet-sized safari park where beasts rule. And you, like any other living creature, are never out of danger if there's something bigger and hungrier lurking nearby.

Which, of course, there is...

That gentle, timid beast over there can't be a threat, surely? It looks like a horse with camel's fur and a nose shaped like a windsock. It goes by the name **Macrauchenia** and I *know* it won't hurt me. But I still feel like I'm being watched...

Suddenly, a stocky shape bounds up from the long grass, aiming straight for Macrauchenia. This is **Smilodon**, a sabre-toothed cat with teeth like carving knives, and it's not alone.

As Macrauchenia is brought to the ground, you run in the other direction. You know you have only a few minutes' head start. The Macrauchenia's already too weak to fight — now it's just meat to fill Smilodon's belly...

A peaceful drink ... but watch out for predators!

49 MILLION YEARS AGO

36 MILLION YEARS AGO

24 MILLION YEARS AGO

3.2 MILLION YEARS AGO

1 MILLION YEARS AGO

30,000 YEARS AGO

BIG BEAR

As you race across the grassy plain, you hear the pounding footfalls of another Smilodon. It sprints after you, the born hunter zeroing in on its prey. Even a single blow from those crushing paws could knock you out ... and you certainly don't want to get too close to those huge fangs.

Smilodon's terrifying smile

But, once again, luck is on your side. A low, throaty roar rings out from the woods ahead of you. Heaving itself into view, comes a shaggy, bear-like beast, **Megatherium**. This is a giant ground **sloth**, the biggest land animal on Earth at this time. It's so big, it could rest its chin on top of a truck, and at the ends of its enormous paws are long talons.

Smilodon hisses at Megatherium and then skulks away in search of easier prey. You breathe a sigh of relief. But what's this strange booming and thudding? It sounds like a gang of giants banging on a massive drum!

49 MILLION YEARS AGO

36 MILLION YEARS AGO

24 MILLION YEARS AGO

3.2 MILLION YEARS AGO

1 MILLION YEARS AGO

30,000 YEARS AGO

One glimpse of Megatherium's lethal-looking claws is enough to make Smilodon forget all about chasing me! Megatherium has nothing to fear from any beast – beneath its skin are tough, bony plates that work like chain mail. Fortunately, the giant sloth barely seems to notice me.

GIANTS CLASH

Investigating the noise, you're left gaping at the sight of yet more massive mammals. Ahead of you are two **Doedicurus**, giant armadillo-like creatures, each the size of a small car. And now you can explain the dreadful din – the animals are battering each other's bony, heavily-armoured bodies. Their weapons are the enormous, spiked clubs that sprout from the ends of their twisting tails.

The two males are fighting over a female Doedicurus, who's shuffling around near the edge of a waterhole. She doesn't seem very interested in who wins the battle, though. Something's caught her eye in the bushes…

With an ear-splitting shriek, a towering mass of feather and muscle tears out of the undergrowth. It's **Phorusrachos**, last of the various terror birds that have been stalking the Earth for over 50 million years. It can't tackle something as big and bony as Doedicurus – but your soft flesh will do very nicely…

Even a terror bird's beak can't crack this shell!

49 MILLION YEARS AGO

36 MILLION YEARS AGO

24 MILLION YEARS AGO

3.2 MILLION YEARS AGO

1 MILLION YEARS AGO

30,000 YEARS AGO

MAMMOTH JOURNEY

You are about to experience the world as it was 30,000 years ago, in the grip of an ice age. Even on a mild day, temperatures won't rise much higher than 10°C – below freezing, that is!

You see some magnificent **Mammoths** approaching over the brow of a hill, their tusks curling out like enormous horns from either side of their trunks. These beasts can survive the cold – underneath their long straggly coats of hair, they have a thick layer of fat that keeps their body temperature stable.

You hear a clattering noise. Two **Giant Elks** are in combat – and they're too busy to notice the pack of hunters creeping up on them. These are your ancestors, **Cro-Magnon Man**. They charge, batter the Elks' heads and bring them down. The men act quickly to strip the animals of meat. They take the bones to carve into tools.

Cro-Magnon hunters charge at a Giant Elk

I don't feel like meeting my ancestors now that they're covered in bits of Elk meat! I think I'll follow the Mammoth herd instead. I wonder where it's going...

49 MILLION YEARS AGO

36 MILLION YEARS AGO

24 MILLION YEARS AGO

3.2 MILLION YEARS AGO

1 MILLION YEARS AGO

30,000 YEARS AGO

BRUTAL HUNT

You drift through the next few months with the Mammoths as they move south. There are many perils along the way, but at last the herd reaches warmer lands. Even here, though, there is a sprinkling of snow on the ground.

You spy several **Woolly Rhinos** grazing happily.

Like a modern rhino – but with hair!

Neanderthals have appeared carrying flaming torches. The flames hide the edge of the cliff — and the Mammoths, trying to escape from the fire, are being driven over the edge. What a horrible, violent death!

The huge horns on their heads come in handy for sweeping away the snow from their grazing lands.

As summer comes, the Mammoths head north again – they need to find more food to sustain the expanding herd. And their great journey brings them into deadly danger from another type of prehistoric human – the **Neanderthals**.

Unlike Cro-Magnon Man, the Neanderthals stay in the same place all the time. Instead of following the herds, they depend on the Mammoths travelling past each year for food and tools.

Neanderthals have invented a horrific way of hunting the giant beasts ... the hairy savages build huge bonfires on a cliff edge. At night, they drive the Mammoths towards the fires so that the animals become confused. What's going to happen to the poor beasts?

49 MILLION YEARS AGO

36 MILLION YEARS AGO

24 MILLION YEARS AGO

3.2 MILLION YEARS AGO

1 MILLION YEARS AGO

30,000 YEARS AGO

SURVIVAL

The brutality of the Mammoth hunt leaves you feeling disturbed. But this is a world where food is scarce and the climate extreme, with no guarantees of staying alive from one day to the next. The Neanderthals have learned, from bitter experience, to kill or be killed.

Staying alive is all that matters, and our ancestors are already finding ways to increase their chances of survival. These Neanderthals won't make it, though. Some day the Mammoths will take a different route north, and this particular group of humans will lose its food source and die out.

Instead of staying put like the Neanderthals, Cro-Magnon hunters follow the herds. This makes life more difficult and dangerous, but it means that, in the end, Cro-Magnon Man will survive.

49 MILLION YEARS AGO

36 MILLION YEARS AGO

24 MILLION YEARS AGO

3.2 MILLION YEARS AGO

1 MILLION YEARS AGO

30,000 YEARS AGO

You drift back to the present. You may not have to struggle as your ancestors did, but modern beasts are *still* fighting tooth and claw – just to stay alive. They always have. And they always will.

FACT FILE

Here are some facts and figures about the most awesome beasts you met on your incredible journey through time...

Basilosaurus

Weight   60 tonnes
Length   20 metres

This ferocious, aquatic powerhouse had a two-metre long skull and a total body length equivalent to three elephants. It was the most feared creature in prehistoric waters.

Andrewsarchus

Weight   250 kilograms
Length   5 metres

With the looks of a wolf but the size of a rhino, Andrewsarchus was a terrifying scavenger. This cruel carnivore stalked the land, preying on the weak, the dying and the dead.

Gastornis

Weight   100 kilograms
Height   1.75 metres

A flightless terror bird as tall as a grown man, Gastornis was a relative of the dinosaurs. It would lie in wait for passing animals, then spring out and grab them in its lethal jaws.

Ambulocetus

Weight   300 kilograms
Length   3 metres

This whale-like predator lurked at lake shorelines waiting for an unwary animal to come near — it then grabbed, drowned and devoured the animal, its rows of teeth shearing through flesh and bone.

Doedicurus

Weight   1,400 kilograms

Length   4 metres

The most heavily-armoured plant-eater ever to have lived. The hard plates rippling over its massive body could resist any attack. Battering this beast with a sledgehammer wouldn't even have made a dent!

Indricothere

Weight   15 tonnes

Height   6 metres

The largest land mammal ever to have existed, Indricothere was a gentle giant. Its towering height allowed it to munch leaves from the treetops.

Smilodon

Weight   240 kilograms

Length   1.5 metres

Smilodon was a mighty, sabre-toothed cat, a cunning killer of the ancient plains. This predator lay in wait and then ambushed its enemies – before tearing them apart.

Chalicothere

Weight   350 kilograms

Height   2.5 metres

Lumbering along with its hairy knuckles pressing on the forest floor, Chalicothere was always looking for food. Its large stomach meant that it had to eat a third of its own body weight each day to survive.

Mammoth

Weight   4–6 tonnes

Height   3 metres

Woolly mammoths had thick, dark hair to protect them from the cold, and long, curved tusks to see off attack. They had huge appetites and were constantly on the move in search of food.

GLOSSARY

Ambulocetus (am-byu-lo-SEE-tus)
A very early whale that was clumsy on land but graceful in the water. It hunted like a crocodile and lived around 49 million years ago.

Andrewsarchus (and-rooz-ARK-uss)
A meat-eater that resembled an outsized wolf. It scavenged on the plains around 36 million years ago.

Apidium (ay-PID-ee-UM)
A lemur-like monkey that lived in troops. It fed on meat and plants found in swamps and forests around 36 million years ago.

Australopithecus (aw-STRAL-uh-PITH-I-cus)
A hairy, human-like ape that slept in trees and moved around on its back legs. It lived mainly on fruit, around 3 million years ago.

Basilosaurus (BAZ-il-uh-SAW-rus)
An early kind of whale. Lacking a blowhole for breathing, Basilosaurus would rest with its head sticking out of the water and tail pointing downwards. It fed on fish, sharks and other marine life, and lived around 36 million years ago.

Brontothere (BRON-tuh-theer)
An animal that looked like a rhino and had a very small brain. It lived and grazed around 36 million years ago.

Chalicothere (KAL-ik-oh-theer)
A browsing animal that looked part-camel, part-panda. Its long arms reached up to strip the tallest branches of leaves. If attacked, it could fight back with lethal claws. It lived around 25 million years ago.

Cro-Magnon Man (kroh-MAG-non man)
An ancestor of Modern Man, Cro-Magnon Man had his own basic language and culture. He hunted with spears and nets around 30,000 years ago.

Deinotherium (dy-noh-THEER-ee-um)
An early elephant with tusks that turned backwards, possibly for stripping bark from trees. It roamed the plains around three million years ago.

Dinofelis (dy-noh-FEE-liss)
A cougar-like big cat that hunted alone and mainly at night. It preyed on other animals, around three million years ago.

Dinosaur (DY-noh-sawr)
A kind of reptile that walked on land more than 65 million years ago but became extinct (died out). The word "dinosaur" means "terrible reptile". Dinosaurs ruled as the major life form on Earth for around 160 million years.

Doedicurus (dee-dik-YOO-russ)
A giant, armoured armadillo, whose rigid tail was solid bone. It grazed on low-lying vegetation around one million years ago.

Dorudon (dor-UH-don)
A mid-sized early whale that looked a little like a dolphin. It lived in small groups, around 24 million years ago.

Entelodont (en-TELL-oh-dont)
An enormous, pig-like scavenger that dominated the plains around 24 million years ago.

Gastornis (gas-TOR-niss)
A flightless bird that stood 1.75 metres tall. This meat-eater may not have been fast, but it was strong and stocky. It lived around 49 million years ago.

Giant Elk
A giant deer with a shaggy mane and huge antlers. It lived around 30,000 years ago.

Hyaenodon (hi-EE-noh-don)
A big-jawed scavenger that preyed on anything smaller that itself, around 24 million years ago.

Indricothere (IN-drik-oh-theer)
A giant cross between a rhino and a giraffe. It grazed on treetops around 24 million years ago.

Leptictidium (LEP-tikt-ID-ee-um)
An agile, shrew-like mammal that hopped around, feeding on insects. It lived around 49 million years ago.

Macrauchenia (mak-row-CHEEN-ee-ah)
A floppy-nosed, camel-like animal that grazed on the plains around one million years ago.

Mammal (MAMM-ul)
A warm-blooded animal that gives birth to live young. Whales, rodents, bears, dogs, cats and humans are all examples of mammals.

Mammoth (MAMM-oth)
A shaggy-haired, elephant-like creature that lived in large herds, around 30,000 years ago.

Megatherium (meg-ah-THEER-ee-um)
A giant ground sloth that mostly grazed on vegetation, but which would occasionally scavenge meat from corpses. It lived around one million years ago.

Moeritherium (mee-ri-THEER-ee-um)
An early elephant with a very short trunk. It lived mostly in water, around 36 million years ago.

Neanderthal (nee-AND-er-thall)
An early human, stockier and less intelligent than Modern Man. It gathered in large groups to hunt its prey around 30,000 years ago.

Phorusrachos (FOR-us-RAK-us)
A fast-running, meat-eating bird with a slim, sharp beak. It hunted around one million years ago.

Propalaeotherium (PROP-al-ay-uh-THEER-ee-um)
A cat-sized ancestor of the modern horse that lived around 49 million years ago.

Smilodon (SMY-loh-don)
A sabre-toothed big cat that used its heavy paws to crush the life out of its victims before feeding. It hunted around one million years ago.

Scavenger
An animal that eats the left-overs of predators' kills.

Sloth
A slow-moving tropical mammal that hangs upside down from the branches of trees using its long limbs and hooked claws.

Woolly Rhino (WOO-lee RYE-noh)
A shaggy-haired rhino with a pair of enormous horns on its snout. It grazed on grass and flowers around 30,000 years ago.

Published by BBC Worldwide Ltd
Woodlands, 80 Wood Lane, London W12 OTT
Text by Stephen Cole © BBC Worldwide Ltd 2001
BBC commissioned photographs © 2000 BBC Worldwide Ltd
Walking with Beasts word mark and logo are
trademarks of the British Broadcasting Corporation
Printed and bound in Singapore
ISBN 0 563 53304 8